Listen First

FOCUSED LISTENING TASKS
FOR BEGINNERS

Jayme Adelson-Goldstein

Oxford University Press

Oxford University Press

200 Madison Avenue
New York, NY 10016 USA

Walton Street
Oxford OX2 6DP England

OXFORD is a trademark of Oxford University Press

ISBN 0-19-434422-3

Acquisitions Editor: Susan Lanzano
Senior Editor: Ellen Lehrburger
Assistant Editor: Paul Phillips
Designer: April Okano
Art Buyer/Picture Researcher: Paula Radding
Production Controller: Abram Hall

Illustrators: Daniel Baxter, Paulette Bogan, Yvonne Buchanan, Nelle Davis,
Eldon Doty, Deborah Drummond, Maj-Britt Hagsted, Stephanie O'Shaughnessy,
Elivia Savadier, and Stephan Van Litsenborg.

Printing (last digit): 10 9 8 7 6 5 4 3

Printed in Hong Kong

Acknowledgments

Loving thanks to Ruthye and Marvin Adelson, for their inspirational insistence that I learn to listen; Susan Lanzano and Ellen Lehrburger, who gave support, delete marks, and friendship; Joanne Abing, Ann Creighton, Kay Devonshire, Vida Hellmann, Sadae Iwataki, and Greta Kojima, friends and professionals all. Grateful acknowledgments go to Paul Phillips, Assistant Editor, April Okano, Designer, and the 1A and 1B ESL students of Evans and North Hollywood Community Adult Schools. Above all, however, I'd like to thank the people whose patience and love made it possible for *Listen First* to be "heard": Gary and Emily Goldstein.

Introduction

Listen First provides beginning-level, adult and young adult ESL students with communicative listening skills through focused listening tasks. These tasks teach students how to listen, clarify, and respond in typical interactive listening situations. They focus on content areas that reinforce zero-level ESL classroom instruction. Material is recycled from unit to unit, ensuring student comprehension and progress.

Beginning-level students are often overwhelmed when they try to understand every word they hear. The exercises in *Listen First* get students to focus on specific information and screen out irrelevant material. Passages are short so that students will focus on comprehension rather than memorization. Nonverbal responses, such as circling, checking, and underlining, enable students to demonstrate their listening skills, even at the earliest stage of language learning. Oral production is preceded by numerous passive and active listening exercises and is carefully scaled to the beginner's level.

Each of the ten units of *Listen First* is divided into seven sections:

See It	an overview of content and vocabulary
Choose It	discrimination activities
Write It	spelling and/or word dictations
Expand It	listening tasks featuring new situations in the content area
Apply It	listening tasks with an emphasis on life skills
Get It Across	dialogue, intonation, and interactive activities
Check It	evaluation activities

Listen First Teacher's Book contains prelistening activities that set up lessons, suggested procedures, and follow-up activities. Consult *Listen First* Teacher's Book for a thorough, section by section treatment of each unit, answer keys, and a complete tapescript.

PRELISTENING

Before students begin working on a unit, they will need some exposure to its context and vocabulary. By starting with prelistening activities, students are able to focus later on specific listening tasks without the additional distraction of processing new vocabulary. Recommended prelistening activities include Total Physical Response (TPR) commands that use realia or visuals, *yes/no* questions with visuals, a preview of the unit dialogue, or a review of related materials students have already learned. Encourage students to listen beyond the interference of words they don't know or have forgotten. This is one of the most valuable lessons a second language listener can learn.

Students acquire the skills needed for communicative listening much more quickly if they feel successful and see progress from one activity to the next. Before listening to the cassette, assist students in making predictions about the material as a preview activity.

UNIT PAGES

See It

The first page of each unit introduces students to the content and context of the unit. Vocabulary is presented in a listening passage, and clarification strategies are previewed. In section A, students look and listen only. This may need to be played more than once if students are unfamiliar with the material. In sections B and C, students listen and follow directions—pointing to words, pictures, or numbers structured within a context, such as a classroom or a department store. In addition, students circle, underline, mark with an x, and check words, pictures, or numbers in a related context.

These TPR activities are a non-threatening way for students to demonstrate their comprehension. During these activities, assess how much of the content or vocabulary is familiar to students and which items need further review.

Choose It

The second page contains a series of discrimination activities using illustrations or short phrases. Students listen to very short passages and circle, mark with an x, match, check, or number the appropriate illustrations based on the information in the listening passage. In doing so, students must focus on a particular aspect of the passage, for example, the part of the body that hurts, and identify the corresponding word or illustration.

Write It

These exercises give students practice in listening for spelling in the first six units, and for focus words in the last four units. The emphasis is always on comprehension, and word boxes are provided when necessary.

The exercises bear a resemblance to more traditional listening exercises, but instead of listening, writing, and then checking, students should be encouraged to write as they listen, with the assurance that they may hear the tape as often as necessary to complete the exercise.

Expand It

New situations and vocabulary are introduced on the **Expand It** page. Just as in **See It**, previewing new vocabulary will facilitate the listening process. You may choose to work from the text illustrations or with realia to familiarize students with the new ideas. It is not necessary for students to produce the new vocabulary, however, they will need to recognize the new items within the context of the unit.

The tasks are supported by illustrations that set the scene and provide valuable clues to understanding the listening passages. Awareness of visual clues is an essential part of first language listening, and language learners need to remember how to use these cues in second language listening situations. For this reason, picture sequencing and matching activities are often found on the **Expand It** page.

Apply It

The tasks on this page use vocabulary, clarification strategies, and situations from the previous four pages in a life-skill area, such as taking a phone message, making an appointment, or asking for directions. Students use the familiar techniques of checking, circling, and making an x in tasks that mimic real-life exchanges. The material in **Apply It** sets up the dialogue for the interaction activity in **Get It Across** and provides examples of clarification strategies.

The teacher can expand on this section by providing students with listening experiences outside the classroom. For example, a scavenger hunt involving school personnel, a call to Directory Assistance for a phone number, or a message left on an answering machine will assist students in applying the listening skills learned in class to the real world.

Get It Across

Active, successful listening is the goal of *Listen First*. **Get It Across** provides students with valuable practice in interactive listening. The initial exercise is always a listening passage, emphasizing a particular clarification strategy. The second exercise is the model dialogue, allowing students to see the clarification structure in print.

To help students practice clarification, interference is built into these first two exercises. The first time a question is answered in the dialogue, some information is blacked out with the interference symbol ⌁. Various noises are used on the cassette to suggest interference. In the classroom, students can have fun using their own techniques, such as coughing, mumbling, rubbing their mouths, or anything that prevents the listener from being sure about the answer to the question.

For the third exercise, pages A and B contain complementary information. This is an information gap in which students must obtain information from their partner in order to complete a grid or chart, draw missing objects in a picture, or put locations on a map.

We recommend you have half the class look at page A, and the other half look at page B. Have students listen to the cassette for the intonation, clarification, and vocabulary used in the interactive activity. Practice the model dialogue with them, later encouraging them to work on it without you. Pair students, As with Bs, reminding them to look only at their own page when working to complete the information gap. This activity may be done twice, with students pairing up again, taking opposite roles.

Check It

The **Check It** page helps students evaluate their progress in each unit of *Listen First*. The first exercise is similar to those on the **Choose It** page, and the second to exercises in **Apply It**. The last exercise is a TPR activity.

The TPR activity requires students to listen for and demonstrate comprehension in a slightly different way, such as moving, drawing, or filling in a chart. On this last activity, the teacher should encourage students to ask for clarification and may pause and replay the tape as often as necessary. The goal of this activity is for every student to succeed in following directions. This success may come from a variety of sources: students requesting clarification, replaying the cassette, students asking other students for clarification, and teacher or student demonstrations.

The evaluation section is not meant to threaten or discourage the student. Encourage students to have fun with the activity.

FOLLOW-UP

The tasks in *Listen First* lend themselves to numerous follow-up activities. *Listen First* Teacher's Book offers a variety of follow-up activities, as well as hints on pairing students, correcting errors, and evaluating performance.

How To Use Listen First

1. Preview each page's vocabulary and context with students before playing the tape.

2. Present one task at a time.

3. Review the task type (circling, checking, matching, etc.) with the class on the board or overhead projector (OHP).

4. Read or have a student read the directions for the task.

5. Check students' comprehension of the directions.

   > Ask *yes/no* questions: *Are you listening for a number?*
   >
   > Ask *or* questions: *Are you listening for a letter or a number?*
   >
   > Have students restate the focus of the task: *We're listening for the number.*
   >
   > Have students predict the kinds of information they're going to hear: *phone numbers.*

6. Play the example.

7. Stop the tape and go over the example on the board or OHP to check students' accuracy.

   > Have a student do the example and have the class correct it.
   >
   > Have individual students call out their answers and let the class come to a consensus.
   >
   > Circulate around the room and check individual student's work.

8. Play the rest of the exercise, pausing as often as necessary, especially between the first and second items. Repeat Step 7 each time the tape is interrupted.

9. Rewind and play the tape again two to four times for students to review and catch missed items. Point out clues in the exercise and write students' suggestions answers on the board for discussion.

10. Help students evaluate their accuracy by having the class come to a consensus on the answers. In cases where there is no consensus after four or five listenings, supply the correct answers on the board or OHP.

11. Play the tape a final time, enabling students to review the correct answers.

Table of Contents

Unit	Listening Focus	Clarification Strategies
1 *page 1* The Alphabet	letters names	*or* repetition
2 *page 9* Numbers	numbers phone numbers	*Excuse me?*
3 *page 17* A Classroom	locations of objects instructions	*Where?*
4 *page 25* Time/A House	time rooms in a house phone messages	rephrasing
5 *page 33* A Department Store	descriptions of clothing prices	*How much?*
6 *page 41* A Neighborhood	locations of buildings directions	*Which?*
7 *page 49* Health	parts of the body symptoms doctor's appointments	*What?*
8 *page 57* The Calendar	dates birthdays	*Wh- questions*
9 *page 65* Employment	occupations work schedules skills	*Wh- questions*
10 *page 73* TheWeather	weather the temperature likes and dislikes	*Wh- questions* rephrasing

page 82	Alphabet Cards	*page 86*	Number Cards

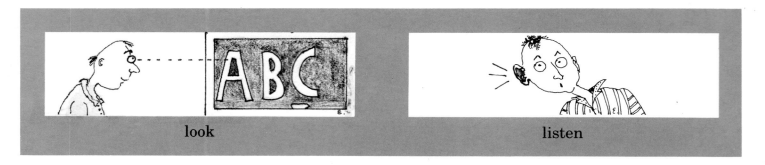

look

listen

A   Look and listen.

A B C D E F G H I J K L M

N O P Q R S T U V W X Y Z

alphabet

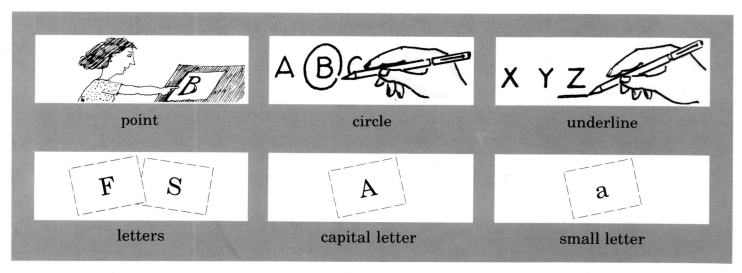

point

circle

underline

letters

capital letter

small letter

B   Point to the letters.
Circle or underline the letters.

A B C D E F G H I J K L M
a b c d e f g h i j k l m

N O P Q R S T U V W X Y Z
n o p q r s t u v w x y z

1

Circle the letter.

1. ⓒ O

2. V W

3. U V

4. L R

5. F S

6. K Q

7. A H

8. I Y

9. B V

10. G J

11. S X

12. N M

2

Underline the letter.

1. L <u>l</u>

2. z Z

3. C c

4. B b

5. E e

6. G j

7. c z

8. k Q

9. C S

10. m w

11. S Z

12. n m

Unit 1
Write It

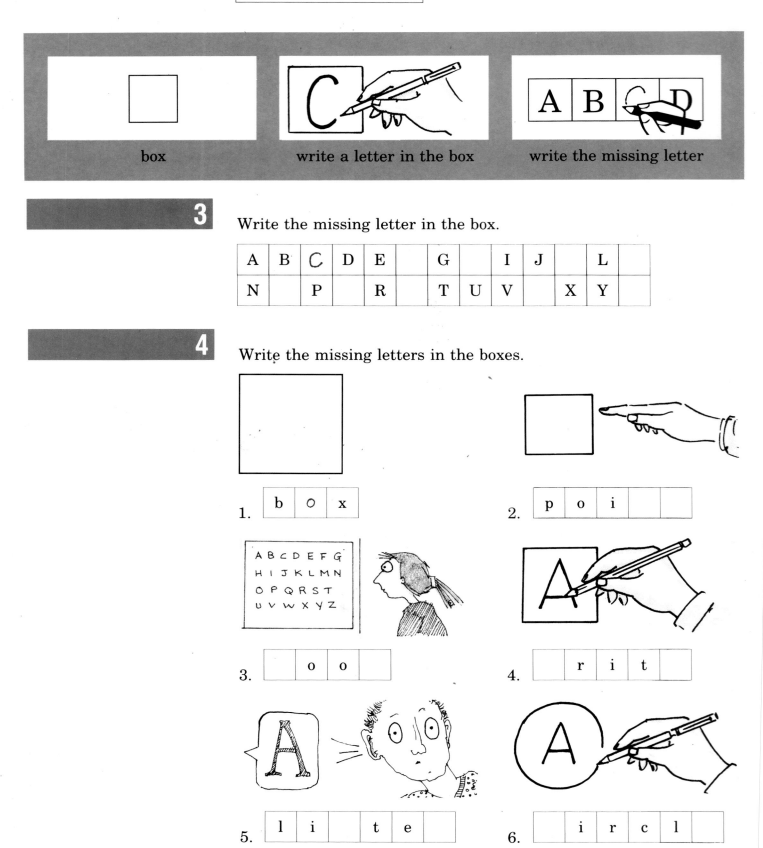

box

write a letter in the box

write the missing letter

3 Write the missing letter in the box.

A	B	C	D	E		G		I	J		L	
N		P		R		T	U	V		X	Y	

4 Write the missing letters in the boxes.

1. | b | o | x |

2. | p | o | i | |

3. | | o | o | |

4. | | r | i | t | |

5. | l | i | | t | e |

6. | | i | r | c | l | |

3

vowels

5 Circle or underline the vowel you hear.

1. <u>A</u> E   2. I E   3. U I

4. I E   5. O E   6. I A

7. U O   8. E A   9. A E

on the line

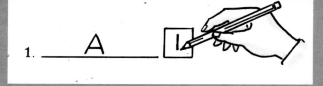

in the box

6 Write the vowel on the line or in the box.

1. _____A_____ [ ]   2. _____ [ ]   3. _____ [ ]

4. _____ [ ]   5. _____ [ ]   6. _____ [ ]

7 Write the letters on the line and in the box.

1. _____B_____ [V]   2. _____ [ ]   3. _____ [ ]

4. _____ [ ]   5. _____ [ ]   6. _____ [ ]

8 Look and listen.

VICTOR   ANTONIO   GOMEZ
first   middle   last

9 Circle the correct letter.

1. (a.) Maria
   b. Mary
   c. Marie

2. a. Martin
   b. Mark
   c. Marvin

3. a. Anne
   b. Ana
   c. Annie

4. a. Mr. Ling
   b. Mr. Lee
   c. Mr. Lu

print your name

sign your name

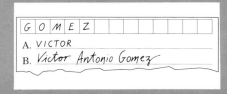

G	O	M	E	Z						

A. VICTOR
B. Victor Antonio Gomez

complete the form

10 Complete the form.

A. _____

B. _____

11

Look and listen.

12

Practice.

Student 1: Point to ⌇⌇⌇.
Student 2: X?
Student 1: No, S.
Student 2: Here it is. S.

13

Say, "Point to . . . ."

G
R
E
L
D
J
A
T

Point to the letters you hear.

11

Look and listen.

12

Practice.

Student 1: Point to ⌒⌒.
Student 2: X?
Student 1: No, S.
Student 2: Here it is. S.

13

Point to the letters you hear.

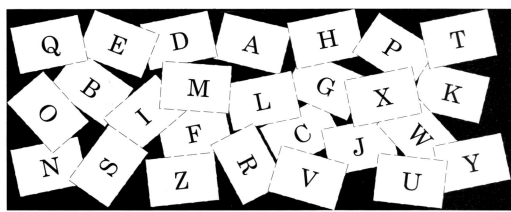

Say, "Point to . . . ."

Q
V
X
E
S
K
B
I

14   Circle or underline the letter.

1. A E   2. A I   3. A H   4. B V   5. B D

6. B P   7. C S   8. J Y   9. D T   10. C Z

15   Write the missing names.

1. _____   2. _____   3. _____ Li

4. _____ Sanchez   5. _____ Alyarak   6. Charles _____

16   Complete the form.

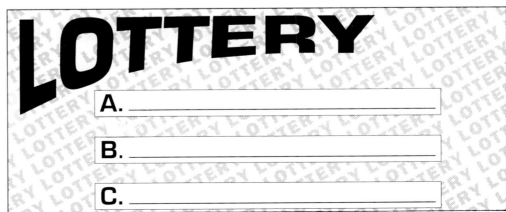

A Look.

0 1 2 3 4 5

6 7 8 9 10

number

word

make an x

B Point to the numbers.
Point to the words.
Make an x.

0 1 2 3 4 5

zero one two three four five

6 7 8 9 10

six seven eight nine ten

Unit 2
Choose It

1 Circle the number you hear.

1. 4 ⑧ 2   2. 9 8 3

3. 0 10 1   4. 7 5 2

5. 6 9 3   6. 2 7 5

2 Make an x in the correct box.

1.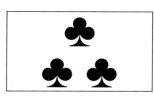

        a.   b.   c.

2.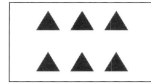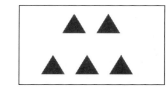

        a.   b.   c.

3.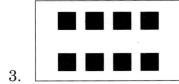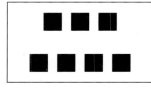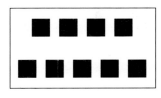

        a.   b.   c.

4.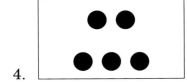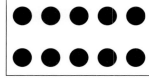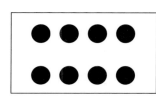

        a.   b.   c.

5.

        a.   b.   c.

3

Write the number you hear.

1. __3__   2. _____   3. _____
4. _____   5. _____   6. _____
7. _____   8. _____   9. _____

4

Write the word.

1. __t h r e e__   2. __ __ __ __ __
3. __ __ __ __ __   4. __ __ __ __ __
5. __ __ __ __ __   6. __ __ __ __ __
7. __ __ __ __ __   8. __ __ __ __ __
9. __ __ __ __   10. __ __ __ __ __

numbers in order   the next number

5 Circle the next number.

1. ③ 2   1   2. 6   8   7
3. 7   5   9   4. 4   5   6
5. 1   10 4   6. 8   9   10
7. 3   6   4   8. 6   7   8
9. 5   7   4   10. 10 0   1

6 Write the next number in the box.

1. [3]   2. [ ]   3. [ ]

4. [ ]   5. [ ]   6. [ ]

7. [ ]   8. [ ]   9. [ ]

10. [ ]   11. [ ]   12. [ ]

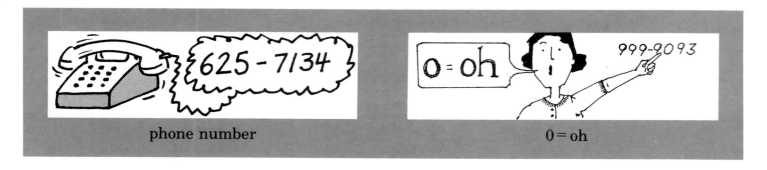

phone number

0 = oh

7 Listen to the phone numbers.

1. 671-8997 2. 312-4655 3. 549-2318 4. 990-7324

8 Write the missing numbers.

1. 625-__7__134   2. 90____-7439   3. 784-8____42

4. ____96-012____   5. 6____1-____294   6. 99____-_____94

a mistake

9 Circle the mistake.

1. 559-690③   2. 483-0207   3. 685-0901

4. 372-6586   5. 421-6230   6. 756-2113

7. 908-3635   8. 555-9899   9. 625-6649

10   Look and listen.

11   Practice.

Student 1:   5   7   ∿.
Student 2:   5   7   9?
Student 1:   No. 5   7   10. Show me.
Student 2:   5   7   10.
Student 1:   Uh-huh.

12   Say, 3   6   9.
           1   3   5.
           4   8   10.
           5   2   7.
Point to the numbers you hear.

10

Look and listen.

11

Practice.

Student 1: 5   7   〜.
Student 2: 5   7   9?
Student 1: No. 5   7   10. Show me.
Student 2: 5   7   10.
Student 1: Uh-huh.

12

Point to the numbers you hear.

Say, 2   4   6.
    0   10   9.
    3   7   4.
    1   8   5.

15

13 Circle the correct number.

1.
5   four   [dots]

2.
zero   [dots]   1

3.
9   three   [dots]

4.
•   4   ten

14 Write the next number.

1. [ ]   2. [ ]   3. [ ]

4. [ ]   5. [ ]   6. [ ]

15 Circle the phone number you hear.

1. 555-1211   555-1212   2. 698-9573   689-9573

3. 413-9035   413-0935   4. 327-0965   237-0965

5. 888-8148   888-8158   6. 997-3143   997-4133

16 Complete the form.

APPLICATION FORM
1. _____
2. _____
3. _____

A

Look.

1. a book

2. a pencil

3. paper

4. a clock

5. a student

6. a teacher

7. a pen

8. a picture of a pen

B

Point to the pencils.

1. next to   2. on   3. under   4. above   5. in

C

Look at the classroom.
Circle the words you hear.

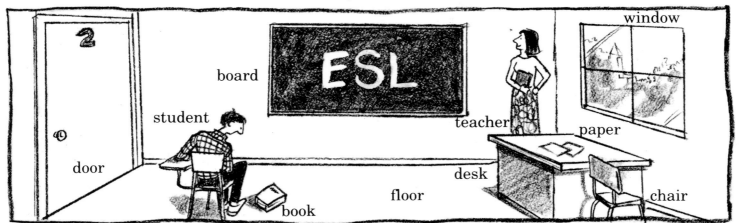

a classroom

Unit 3
Choose It

1 Make an x on the correct letter.

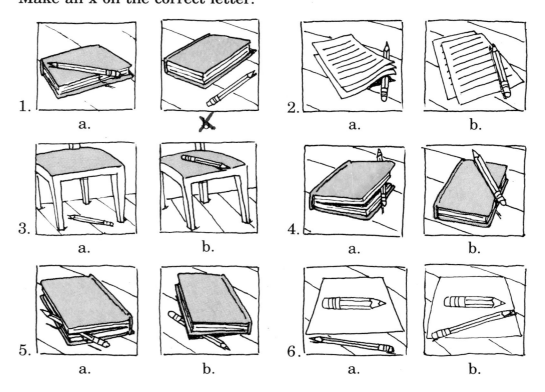

1.
  a.
  X

2.
  a.
  b.

3.
  a.
  b.

4.
  a.
  b.

5.
  a.
  b.

6.
  a.
  b.

2 Put the numbers on the picture.

3 Write the missing words.

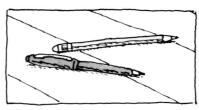

1. The pen is n e x t   t o the pencil.

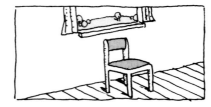

2. The window is ___ ___ ___ ___ ___ the chair.

3. The pen is ___ ___ ___ ___ ___ the book.

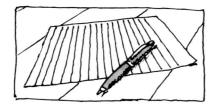

4. The pen is ___ ___ the paper.

4 Write the words next to the pictures.

door

19

on the left   on the right

5 Look and listen.

1.   2.   3.

4.   5.   6. pencil

draw   make a √

6 Draw and make a √.

1.   2.   3.

7 Circle the letter under the correct picture.

1. ⓐ   b.   2. a.   b.

3. a.   b.   4. a.   b.

8 Look at the picture. Make a ✓ under the correct answer.

	above the box	under the box	next to the box, on the left	next to the box, on the right	on the box
1.			✓		
2.					
3.					
4.					
5.					

9 Look and listen.

10 Practice.

Student 1: Where's the chair?
Student 2: It's next to the board, on the ⌇.
Student 1: On the left or on the right?
Student 2: On the left.

11 Ask, "Where's the . . . ?"

        pen
        window
        5
        paper

22

9   Look and listen.

10   Practice.

Student 1:   Where's the chair?
Student 2:   It's next to the board, on the ∾.
Student 1:   On the left or on the right?
Student 2:   On the left.

11   Ask, "Where's the . . . ?"

          teacher
          pencil
          1
          book

12 Circle the letter under the correct picture.

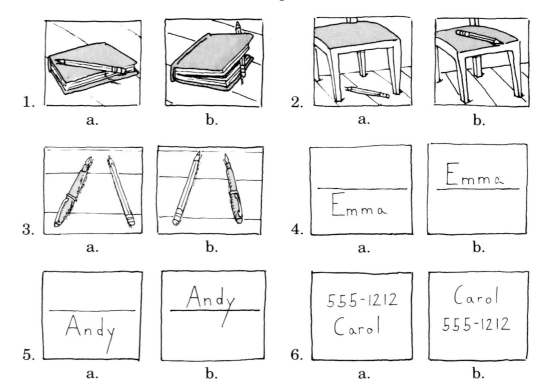

1. a. b.   2. a. b.

3. a. b.   4. a. b.

5. a. b.   6. a. b.

13 Make a √ or an x. Draw a line or a circle.

N	Q	V	K	D
O	J	T	R	U
V	C	Z	H	I
A	I	X	K	B
S	E	F	A	E

14 Do it.

Point to your book.

A

Look.

1. 1:00   2. 1:05   3. 1:15   4. 1:30

B

Look.
Point to the numbers.

11	12	13	14	15	16	17	18	19
20	21	22	23	24	25	26	27	28	29
30	40	50	60	70	80	90	100		

C

Make an x.

1. at work

2. at home

3. the living room

4. the kitchen

5. the bathroom

6. the bedroom

1

Make a √ on the number you hear.

1. 5   15   50   2. 12   20   22   3. 6   16   60

4. 4   14   40   5. 7   17   70   6. 3   13   30

7. 9   19   90   8. 10   11   100   9. 8   18   80

the correct time

2

Circle the letter under the correct time.

1.

    a.   b.   (c.)

2.

    a.   b.   c.

3.

    a.   b.   c.

4.

    a.   b.   c.

5.

    a.   b.   c.

6.

    a.   b.   c.

digital clock

3 Write the missing numbers on the clocks.

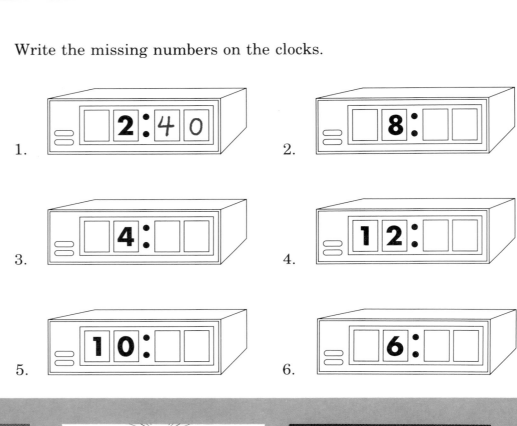

1. **2:40**

2. **8:**

3. **4:**

4. **12:**

5. **10:**

6. **6:**

Good morning.

Good afternoon.

Good evening.

greetings

4 Write a.m. or p.m. next to the time.

1. It's 6:00 *a.m.*

2. It's 3:00 _____

3. It's 6:00 _____

4. It's 5:00 _____

5. It's 10:45 _____

6. It's 8:30 _____

5

Write the time on the clocks.

1.

2.

3.

4.

5.

6.

6

Listen to the questions and look at the pictures above.
Circle yes or no.

1. yes (no)   2. yes   no   3. yes   no   4. yes   no

5. yes   no   6. yes   no   7. yes   no   8. yes   no

7

Write the correct numbers on the pictures.

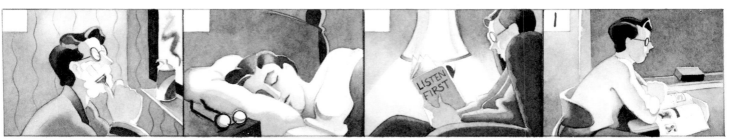

leave a message   take a message

8 Listen to the phone conversations and look at the messages.

☎ ☎ ☎ ☎ ☎ ☎
Telephone Message

Time: *4:00*

Call: *Rick Green at home*

Number: *550-4321*

☎ ☎ ☎ ☎ ☎ ☎
Telephone Message

Time: *4:30*

Call: *Ken at work*

Number: *773-0980*

9 Take the messages.

☎ ☎ ☎ ☎ ☎ ☎
Telephone Message

Time: _____

Call: _____

_____

Number: _____

1.

☎ ☎ ☎ ☎ ☎ ☎
Telephone Message

Time: _____

Call: _____

_____

Number: _____

2.

10 Look and listen.

11 Practice.

Student 1: Hello. Is Ed there?
Student 2: No, he isn't. May I take a message?
Student 1: This is David. I'm at home. My number is 684-0821.
Student 2: Call David at home, 684-0821.
Student 1: That's right. Thank you. Bye.
Student 2: Bye.

12 Listen to your partner.
Take the message for Kate.

Message pad for Kate!

Time: _____

Kate, call: _____

at: _____

Phone number: _____

Call your partner. Ask for Arnold.
Leave a message for Arnold.

> You are at work.
> Your phone number is 956-3121.

10 Look and listen.

11 Practice.

Student 1: Hello. Is Ed there?
Student 2: No, he isn't. May I take a message?
Student 1: This is David. I'm at home. My number is 684-0821.
Student 2: Call David at home, 684-0821.
Student 1: That's right. Thank you. Bye.
Student 2: Bye.

12 Call your partner. Ask for Kate.
Leave a message for Kate.

You are at home.
Your phone number is 317-1954.

Listen to your partner.
Take the message for Arnold.

Message pad for Arnold!

Time: _____

Arnold, call: _____

at: _____

Phone number: _____

13 Look at the pictures. Write the correct numbers in the boxes.

14 Take the message.

☎ ☎ ☎ ☎ ☎ ☎
Telephone Message

Time: _____

Call: _____

_____

Number: _____

1.

☎ ☎ ☎ ☎ ☎ ☎
Telephone Message

Time: _____

Call: _____

_____

Number: _____

2.

15 Do it.

Unit 5
See It

A

Look.

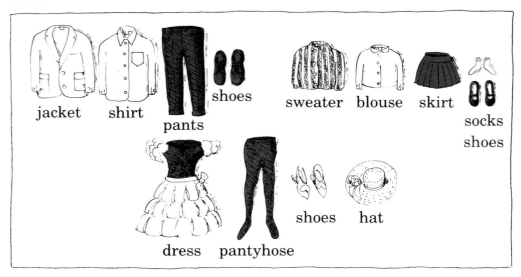

jacket　　shirt　　shoes　　sweater　　blouse　　skirt　　socks shoes

pants

dress　　pantyhose　　shoes　　hat

B

Look at the department store.
Point to the words you hear.

department store

C

Look.
Make a √ above the picture.

1.

2.

3.

4.

1

Circle the letter under the correct picture.

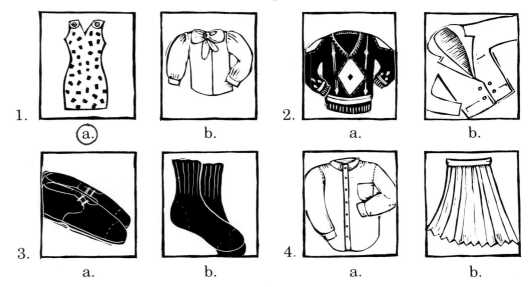

1.
   (a.)   b.

2.
   a.   b.

3.
   a.   b.

4.
   a.   b.

2

Make a √ next to the words you hear.

1. ✓ shirt   2. ____ sweater   3. ____ jacket   4. ____ blouse

   ____ dress   ____ pants   ____ shirt   ____ skirt

   ✓ shoes   ____ socks   ____ skirt   ____ pantyhose

3

Draw a line from the name to the correct picture.

1. George   2. Hannah   3. Roy   4. Flora

4 Write the correct words next to the pictures.

jacket ✓
skirt
pants
socks
sweater
dresses

jacket

5 Help Simon write his shopping list.

shopping list	
1	1 jacket
2	
3	
4	pairs of
5	pairs of
6	pair of

shopping list

6 Circle the letter under the correct price.

1. PRICE $30.00 — (a.)   PRICE $13.00 — b.

2. $50.00 — a. $15.00 — b.

3. ONLY $40⁰⁰ — a.   ONLY $14⁰⁰ — b.

4. SALE $60⁰⁰ — a.   SALE $16⁰⁰ — b.

7 Write the prices on the price tags.

1.

2.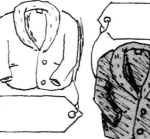

3.

4.

Unit 5
Apply It

8 Make a √ in the correct box.

	👞	👟	skirt	skirt	top	top
on sale 50% off						
on sale 25% off	✓					
regular price						

rest rooms   furniture   restaurant   offices

9 Look at the directory and circle the correct answer.

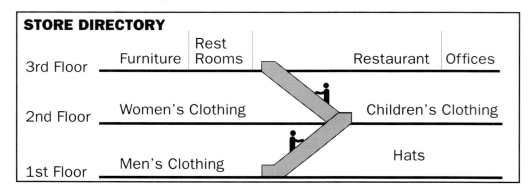

STORE DIRECTORY

3rd Floor	Furniture	Rest Rooms	Restaurant	Offices
2nd Floor	Women's Clothing		Children's Clothing
1st Floor	Men's Clothing		Hats

1. a. 1st floor
   (b.) 2nd floor
   c. 3rd floor

2. a. 1st floor
   b. 2nd floor
   c. 3rd floor

3. a. 1st floor
   b. 2nd floor
   c. 3rd floor

4. a. 1st floor
   b. 2nd floor
   c. 3rd floor

5. a. 1st floor
   b. 2nd floor
   c. 3rd floor

6. a. 1st floor
   b. 2nd floor
   c. 3rd floor

10 Look and listen.

11 Practice.

Student 1: How much is that blouse?
Student 2: Which one?
Student 1: The black one.
Student 2: ∿.
Student 1: How much?
Student 2: $24.00.

12 Ask for the missing prices.

10 Look and listen.

11 Practice.

Student 1: How much is that blouse?
Student 2: Which one?
Student 1: The black one.
Student 2: ∿∿.
Student 1: How much?
Student 2: $24.00.

12 Ask for the missing prices.

13

Make an x, a √, or a circle. Write the correct words or numbers.

1.  2.  3.

14

Write the prices on the receipts.

RECEIPT	
shoes	_____
socks	_____
sweater	_____
pants	_____
shirt	_____
jacket	_____
TOTAL	_____

RECEIPT	
shoes	_____
dress	_____
sweater	_____
blouse	_____
skirt	_____
jacket	_____
TOTAL	_____

15

Do it.

A Look.

bank

park

hospital

supermarket

drugstore

gas station

movie theater

restaurant

B Look at the places.
Point to the addresses.

1. between

2. on the corner of

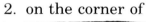

3. around the corner from

4. across from

C Look and point to the places you hear.

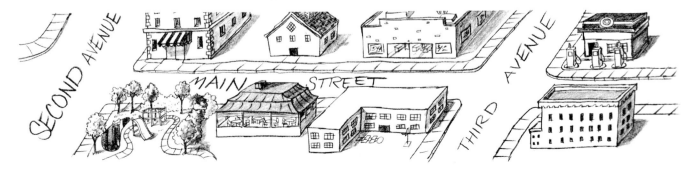

1

Write the correct letter on the line.

_e_ 1.

____ 2.

____ 3.

____ 4.

____ 5.

____ 6.

a. 3930 Green Road   b. 4014 Second Avenue

c. 4012 Second Avenue   d. 3929 Center Street

e. 4041 Center Street   f. 1770 First Avenue

2

Look at the picture. Circle the correct letter.

1. (a.) restaurant   2. a. park   3. a. bank

   b. movie theater   b. apartment building   b. school

4. a. gas station   5. a. drugstore   6. a. bank

   b. movie theater   b. movie theater   b. park

3 Write the words you hear.

1. _School_

2. _____

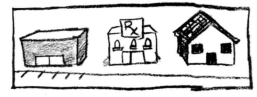

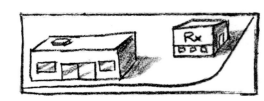

3. _____

4. _____

4 Write the words you hear.

next to ✓
between
across from
on the corner of
around the
corner from

1. The school is _next to_ the park.

2. The restaurant is _____ the drugstore.

3. The gas station is _____ First and Center.

4. The hospital is _____ the supermarket and my house.

5. The supermarket is _____ the park.

43

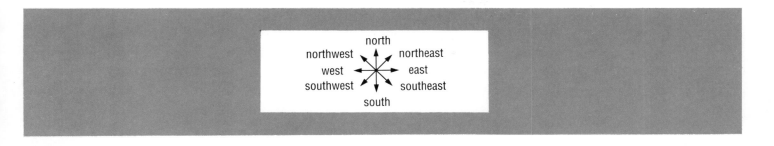

5 Look and listen.

6 Write the correct numbers on the map.

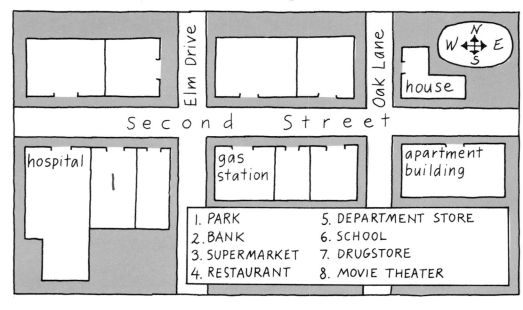

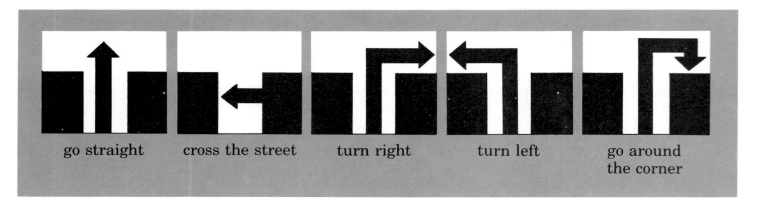

go straight   cross the street   turn right   turn left   go around the corner

7 Make an x under the directions you hear.

1.	×				
2.					
3.					
4.					
5.					

L	R	N	S	E	W	St.	Ave.
left	right	north	south	east	west	street	avenue

abbreviations

8 Use the abbreviations above to write the directions.

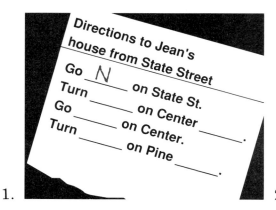

Directions to Jean's house from State Street
Go __N__
Turn _____ on State St.
Go _____ on Center
Turn _____ on Center.
_____ on Pine _____.

1.

Directions to Jean's house from Oak Street and Hill Avenue
Go _____ on Hill _____
to Bay _____.
Turn _____.
Go _____ on Bay.
_____ on Bay to Pine.
Address: 5015 Pine
Apartment 13

2.

9 Look and listen.

10 Practice.

Student 1: Excuse me, where's the bank from here?
Student 2: Walk north on Pine and cross Second.
It's on the ∿ corner.
Student 1: Which corner?
Student 2: The northwest corner.
Student 1: Thanks.

11 Ask your partner for directions to the supermarket.
the drugstore.
the restaurant.
the school.

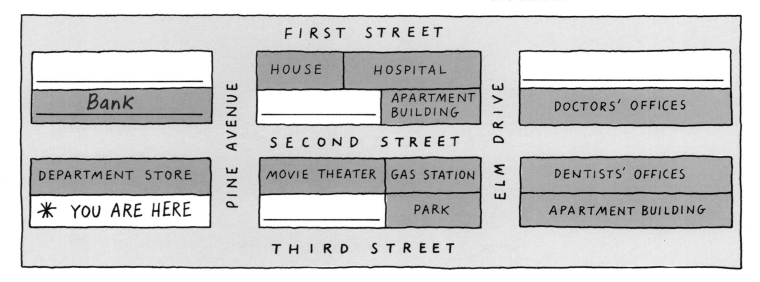

9

Look and listen.

Which corner? The northwest corner.

10

Practice.

Student 1: Excuse me, where's the bank from here?

Student 2: Walk north on Pine and cross Second.
 It's on the ⌒⌒⌒ corner.

Student 1: Which corner?

Student 2: The northwest corner.

Student 1: Thanks.

11

Ask your partner for directions to the park.
the movie theater.
the hospital.
the department store.

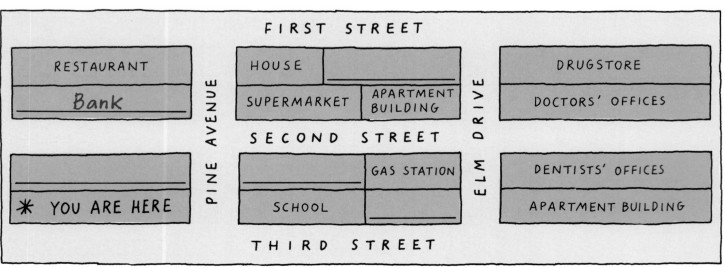

12 Write the correct addresses on the buildings.

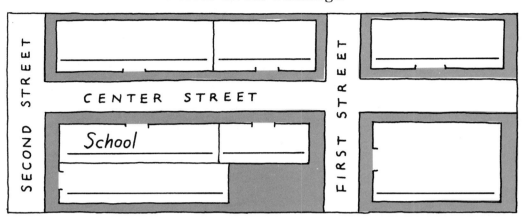

13 Make a √ under the correct location.

	on the left	across from	around the corner from	between	on the right
hospital					
school					
gas station					
restaurant					
supermarket					

14 Do it.

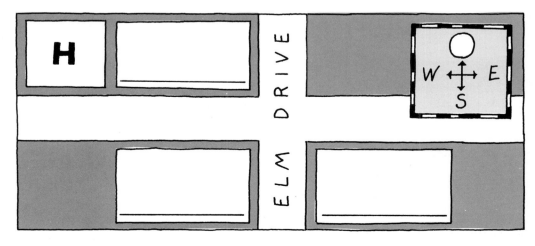

Unit 7
See It

A Look.

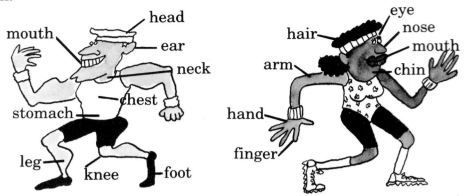

B Look.
Point to the pictures.

1. fine 2. sick 3. a cough 4. a cold

5. a fever 6. a sore throat 7. It hurts.

C Look.
Make a √ under the picture.

1. a backache 2. a stomachache 3. a headache 4. an earache 5. a toothache

1   Circle the letter under the correct picture.

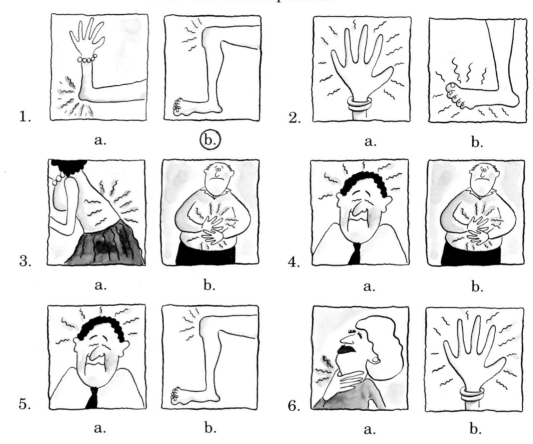

1.
   a.   b.

2.
   a.   b.

3.
   a.   b.

4.
   a.   b.

5.
   a.   b.

6.
   a.   b.

2   Write a number next to the correct part of the body.

3 Write the missing letters or words.

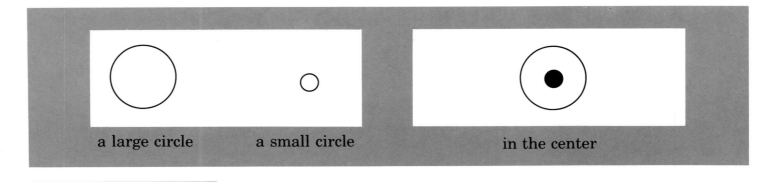

What's the matter?

I have _____.

cold
cough
sore throat ✓
earache
stomachache
backache

1. I have a sore __t__ __h__ __r__ __o__ __a__ __t__ .

2. I have a __ __ __ __ ache.

3. I have a __ __ __ __ __ __ __ ache.

4. I have an __ __ __ ache.

5. I have a __ __ __ __ __ .

6. I have a __ __ __ __ .

a large circle   a small circle   in the center

4 Draw or write what you hear.

1. _____

2. _____

3. _____

Unit 7
Expand It

have → need

5

Look and listen.

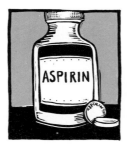   

1. aspirin   2. antacid   3. cough drops   4. a doctor

6

Write the correct letter on the line.

<u>a</u> 1.   ___ 2.   ___ 3.   ___ 4.

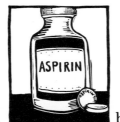 a.  b.  c.  d.

7

Circle yes or no.

1. a. (yes) no   2. a. yes no   3. a. yes no   4. a. yes no
   b. yes no   b. yes no   b. yes no   b. yes no
   c. yes no   c. yes no   c. yes no   c. yes no

make an appointment

8 Make a √ under the correct appointment times.

	9:30	10:45	11:00	11:45	1:45	2:00	4:15
Joe Smith						✓	
Ling Chan							
Jung Kim							
Michiko Suzuki							
Josh Quinn							

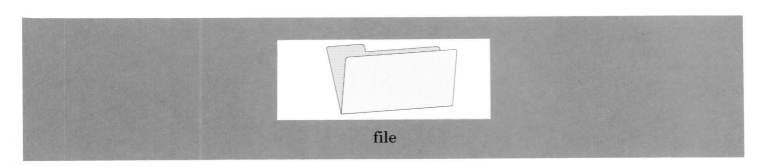

file

9 Look at the files and circle the correct information.

1. Chuck Singh
   (fever)/back   (9:00)/9:15

2. Irene Lopez
   cough/cold   10:30/9:30

3. Vic Carr
   sore throat/sore arm   9:40/9:45

4. Lola Yakamura
   fever/foot   10:15/10:50

5. Joe Green
   ear/eye   10:05/10:45

Unit 7
Get It Across
A

10 Look and listen.

11 Practice.

Student 1: Charles Chan has a 2:00 appointment.
Student 2: What's the matter?
Student 1: He has a ∿.
Student 2: He has a what?
Student 1: A stomachache.

12 Ask and answer questions about the appointments.

Time	Patient	Problem
2:00	Charles Chan	stomachache
2:15	Jane Adams	backache
2:45	Ira Lupino	
3:00	Paul Gomez	fever
4:00	Dae Yong Noh	headache
4:15	Bruce Lee	
5:00	Helen Yoshiro	

10

Look and listen.

11

Practice.

Student 1: Charles Chan has a 2:00 appointment.
Student 2: What's the matter?
Student 1: He has a ∿.
Student 2: He has a what?
Student 1: A stomachache.

12

Ask and answer questions about the appointments.

Time	Patient	Problem
2:00	Charles Chan	Stomachache
2:15	Jane Adams	
2:45	Ira Lupino	sore throat
3:00	Paul Gomez	
4:00	Dae Yong Noh	
4:15	Bruce Lee	earache
5:00	Helen Yoshiro	cough

13 Look at the picture. Draw or write the parts of the body.

14 Make a √ under the problem.

	headache	backache	stomachache	sore throat	cough	cold
1. Carlos						
2. Flora						
3. Nasim						
4. Bertha						
5. Henry						

15 Write the correct letter on the line.

_____ 1. 2:15   a. Mrs. Sanchez' knee

_____ 2. 2:30   b. Mr. Yamamoto's throat

_____ 3. 3:00   c. Mrs. Johnson's back

_____ 4. 3:30   d. Mrs. Carson's foot

_____ 5. 3:45   e. Toshi Suzuki's shoulder

_____ 6. 4:15   f. Mr. Jones' cough

16 Do it.

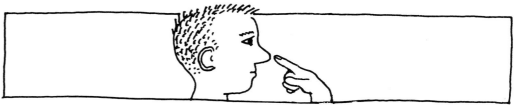

A Look.

October						
Su	M	Tu	W	Th	F	Sa
	1	2	3	4	5	6
7	8	9	10	11	12	13
14	15	16	17	18	19	20
21	22	23	24	25	26	27
28	29	30	31			

1. a calendar

Th	F	Sa
4	5	6

2. yesterday   today   tomorrow

B Look at the week.
Point to the days.

Sunday	Monday	Tuesday	Wednesday	Thursday	Friday	Saturday
	1	2	3	4	5	6

a week

C Look and point.
Look and circle.

Su	M	Tu	W	Th	F	Sa
	1	2	3	4	5	6
7	8	9	10	11	12	13
14	15	16	17	18	19	20
21	22	23	24	25	26	27
28	29	30	31			

a month

1

Make an x in the correct box.

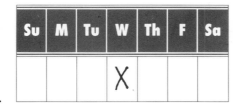

1.

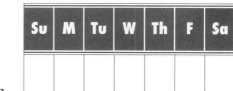

2.

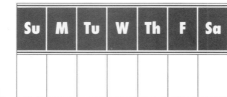

3.

4.

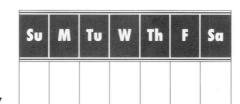

5.

6.

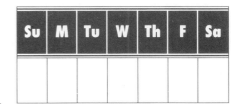

7.

8.

2

Circle the correct date.

Su	M	Tu	W	Th	F	Sa
	1	2	3	4	5	6
(7)	8	9	10	11	12	13
14	15	16	17	18	19	20
21	22	23	24	25	26	27
28	29	30	31			

3 Write the missing days.

```
_____ market _____
_____ doctor _____
_____ party _____
_____ dentist _____ Monday _____
_____ bank _____
_____ movies _____
_____ park _____
_____ gym _____
```

4 Write the missing words.

| yesterday |
| you |
| first |
| Monday |
| today |
| your |
| Tuesday |
| work |
| morning ✓ |
| Sunday |
| last |

Good __morning_____ .

  Good morning! Why are _____
  wearing _____ pajamas?

Why? Because it's _____ .

  It isn't Sunday. It's _____ .

Are you sure?

  Well, _____ was Sunday. Tomorrow
  is _____ . Yes, _____ is
  Monday.

Oh no! I'm late for _____ .

  It's not the _____ time.

Goodbye dear!

  And it won't be the _____ .

5 Look and listen.

January =	**1**	April =	**4**	July =	**7**	October =	**10**
February =	**2**	May =	**5**	August =	**8**	November =	**11**
March =	**3**	June =	**6**	September =	**9**	December =	**12**

6 Circle the correct date.

1. (9/10) 8/9   2. 6/8 8/8   3. 3/12 4/12
4. 1/7 6/1   5. 2/22 4/22   6. 11/9 9/11

7 Write the dates you hear.

1. New Year's Day is __1/1__ .

2. Valentine's Day is _____ .

3. April Fool's Day is _____ .

4. Flag Day is _____ .

5. Independence Day is _____ .

6. Halloween is _____ .

7. Veteran's Day is _____ .

8. Christmas Day is _____ .

birthday

8 Make a √ under the correct birthday.

	1/8	2/10	3/4	4/3	8/1	10/2
Martha				✓		
Freddy						
Surijak						
Gloria						
Michiko						

9 Write the correct letter on the line.

_c_ 1. Helen   a. 12/3/69

_____ 2. Mike   b. 12/3/58

_____ 3. Yasu   c. 12/3/52

_____ 4. Leona   d. 12/3/73

married

1st child

10 Write the correct dates on the time line.

born   last day of school   1st child

1/7/68   1st day of school   married

11 Look and listen.

12 Practice.

Student 1: When's Martha's birthday?
Student 2: It's January ⋀⋀⋀.
Student 1: January what?
Student 2: January 15.

13 Ask your partner for birthdays for Lisa.
Roger.
Myron.
Janet.

JANUARY						
1	2	3	4	5	6	7
8	9	10	11	12	13	14
15 Martha	16	17	18	19	20	21
22	23	24	25 Frank	26	27	28
29	30	31 Shirley				

JUNE						
		1	2	3	4	5
6	7	8	9	10 Laura	11	12
13	14 Paul	15	16	17	18	19
20	21	22	23	24	25	26
27	28	29	30			

11

Look and listen.

12

Practice.

Student 1: When's Martha's birthday?
Student 2: It's January ∿.
Student 1: January what?
Student 2: January 15.

13

Ask your partner for birthdays for Frank.
Paul.
Shirley.
Laura.

JANUARY						
1	2	3	4	5	6	7
8	9	10	11	12	13	14
15 Martha	16	17	18	19	20	21
22	23	24	25	26	27 Lisa	28
29	30	31				

JUNE						
		1	2	3	4	5
6	7 Roger	8	9	10	11	12
13	14	15	16 Myron	17	18	19
20	21	22	23	24	25	26
27	28	29	30 Janet			

14 Make an x next to the correct day.

1. ☐ Monday ☐ Sunday   2. ☐ Saturday ☐ Sunday

3. ☐ Tuesday ☐ Thursday   4. ☐ Thursday ☐ Saturday

5. ☐ Friday ☐ Wednesday   6. ☐ Tuesday ☐ Monday

15 Write the date on the calendar.

NOVEMBER						
Su	M	Tu	W	Th	F	Sa

16 Circle the correct dates.

1. October 1   October 31   2. February 14   February 4

3. 12/25   12/5   4. 6/14   7/2

5. 3/12/56   12/3/56   6. 9/13/30   9/30

17 Do it.

Personal Information Card

_____

_____

_____

_____

A Look.

a computer programmer   a truck driver   a cook   a salesperson

a secretary   an accountant   a factory worker   a plumber

B Look at the employment agency.
Point to the people.

C Look.
Look and circle.

Job Opening	cook
Location	Mario's Pizza
Hours	10:00 a.m. - 6:00 p.m.
Start Date	11/7
Salary	$6.75/hour
Days off	Monday

Job Opening	factory worker
Location	NTC Co.
Hours	7:00 a.m. - 5:00 p.m.
Start Date	11/8
Salary	$7.50/hour
Days off	Sunday

1

Circle the letter under the correct picture.

1.

a.   (b.)

2.

a.   b.

3.

a.   b.

4.

a.   b.

5.

a.   b.

6.

a.   b.

2

Write the correct letter on the line.

__d__ 1. cook   a. $17.00/hour
____ 2. factory worker   b. 11/1
____ 3. plumber   c. 8:00 a.m.–5:00 p.m.
____ 4. truck driver   d. 11/6
____ 5. accountant   e. $7.00/hour
____ 6. secretary   f. 10/30

66

3

Write the missing words.

computer programmer
accountant
plumber
salesperson
secretary ✓

What do those people do?

    Excuse me?

What are their jobs?

    The woman in the center is a ___secretary___ .
    The man next to her, on the right, is an _____ .
    The woman next to her, on the left, is a _____ .
    The woman next to the accountant, on the right,
    is a _____ .
    The man next to the plumber is a _____ .

Why are they standing in line?

    It's their day off. They're all going to the movies.

4

Write the missing words or numbers on the job board.

○	Job	Hours	Salary ○
	cook	10:00 a.m. – 7:00 p.m.	$6.50/hour
	secretary	8:30 a.m. - 5:00 p.m.	$6.75/hour
	computer programmer		
	salesperson	1:30 p.m. - 9:30 p.m.	

Unit 9
Expand It

5 Look and listen.

Can

file

drive a car

use a cash register

speak English

Can't

type

drive a truck

use a computer

speak Chinese

6 Make a √ when you hear **can** and an x when you hear **can't.**

Meg	√	√	√	X	X	X	√
Oscar							
Lorena							
Feng Li							
Toshi							

occupation = job   part-time/full-time   day shift/night shift

7 Circle the correct letter.

1. (a.) Paul Chan 2. a. cook 3. a. full-time 4. a. night shift

    b. Paul Chen   b. clerk   b. part-time   b. day shift

job ad

8 Read the job ads. Circle the correct letter.

1.

COOK NEEDED Mornings Part-time $7.00/hour	**COOK NEEDED** Afternoons Part-time $7.00/hour
a.	(b.)

2.

FACTORY JOBS Day shift Full-time $6.50/hour	**FACTORY JOBS** Night shift Full-time $6.50/hour
a.	b.

3.

SECRETARY WANTED Type, file, phones No computers Full-time	**SECRETARY WANTED** Type, file, phones and computers Full-time
a.	b.

4.

DRIVER WANTED Full-time $6.00/hour	**TRUCK DRIVER WANTED** Full-time $6.00/hour
a.	b.

9 Look and listen.

10 Practice.

Student 1: Tell me about Rob Hall.
Student 2: He's a cook. He can ⌁ and he can ⌁.
Student 1: He can do what?
Student 2: He can cook Chinese food and he can speak English.

11 Ask your partner about Anna and Ted.
Write the information.

Name	Occupation	Skills
Rob Hall	cook	can: cook Chinese food speak English
Anna Ruiz		can:
John Mackie	secretary	can: use a computer speak French
Ted Darrin		can:
Linda Li	plumber	can: fix sinks speak Chinese

9 Look and listen.

10 Practice.

Student 1: Tell me about Rob Hall.
Student 2: He's a cook. He can ∿ and he can ∿.
Student 1: He can do what?
Student 2: He can cook Chinese food and he can speak English.

11 Ask your partner about John and Linda.
Write the information.

Name	Occupation	Skills
Rob Hall	cook	can: cook Chinese food speak English
Anna Ruiz	accountant	can: use a calculator speak Spanish
John Mackie		can:
Ted Darrin	driver	can: drive a truck speak English
Linda Li		can:

12

Circle the letter under the correct picture.

1.
   a.   b.

2.
   a.   b.

3.
   a.   b.

4.
   a.   b.

13

Circle what the people can do, the salary, and hours they want.

1.
Jade Lee	cook
Chinese food	Mexican food
day shift	night shift

2.
Victor Perez	computer programmer
$15.00/hour	$50.00/hour
part-time	full-time

3.
Sue Lanzano	plumber
$20.00/hour	$12.00/hour
part-time	full-time
day shift	night shift

4.
Ray Bean	secretary
type	use a computer
part-time	full-time
day shift	night shift

14

Do it.

Job Form

1._____

2. part-time   full-time

3. day shift   night shift

4. a._____   b._____

5. _____

Unit 10
See It

A Look.

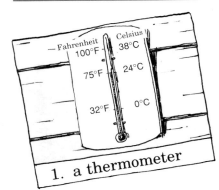

1. a thermometer

Fahrenheit   Celsius
100°F   38°C
75°F   24°C
32°F   0°C

2. cold

3. cool

4. warm

5. hot

B Look at the weather.
Point to the cities.

1. sunny

2. cloudy

3. windy

4. smoggy

5. foggy

6. raining

7. snowing

C Point.
Circle.

1. beach 65°F

2. city 78°F

3. desert 98°F

4. valley 45°F

5. mountains 29°F

73

Unit 10
Choose It

1

Circle the correct letter.

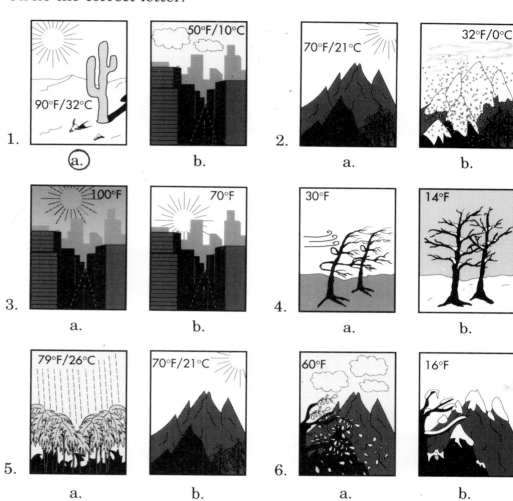

1.
a. (circled)
b.

2.
a.
b.

3.
a.
b.

4.
a.
b.

5.
a.
b.

6.
a.
b.

2

Make a √ next to the correct word.

1. ✓ sunny
   ___ cloudy
   ___ foggy

2. ___ sunny
   ___ cloudy
   ___ foggy

3. ___ raining
   ___ cloudy
   ___ foggy

4. ___ foggy
   ___ cloudy
   ___ smoggy

5. ___ windy
   ___ raining
   ___ foggy

6. ___ cloudy
   ___ foggy
   ___ raining

Unit 10
Write It

3

Write the missing words.

cool
warm ✔
cloudy
sunny
foggy
windy

Here's our weather report for the week.

Today will be _____warm_____ and about 70°.

Sunday will be _____ and 90°.

Monday will be _____ and 92°.

Tuesday will be _____ and 75°.

Wednesday will be _____ and 70°.

Thursday will be _____ and 65°.

Friday will be _____ , with rain in the afternoon and temperatures in the 60's.

4

Write the high and low temperatures.

	city	beach	valley	mountains	desert
High	78°				
Low	45°				

5 Look and listen.

| spring | summer | fall | winter |

6 Write the correct name under the picture.

Jim ✓
Diane
Louise
Buddy

_____   ___Jim___   _____   _____

like

don't like

7 Make a √ when you hear **like.**
Make an x when you hear **don't like.**

	spring	summer	fall	winter
Lily	✓	✓	✓	✗
Gary				
Jordan				
Tanya				

8 Listen and look.

9 Circle the correct letter.

1. a. b.
2. a. b.
3. a. b.
4. a. b.

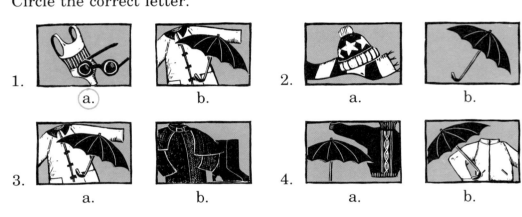

airport closed   road closed

10 Make an x under the airports and roads that are closed.

City	Airport	101	5	10	95
Los Angeles	×			×	
New York					
Miami					
Chicago					
San Francisco					

11

Look and listen.

12

Practice.

Student 1: What's the weather in Los Angeles?
Student 2: It's sunny and warm.
Student 1: What's the temperature?
Student 2: It's 75° Fahrenheit.
Student 1: What's that in Celsius?
Student 2: 24°.

13

Ask your partner for the missing information.

City	Weather	Temperature	
		Fahrenheit	Celsius
Los Angeles	sunny and warm	75°	24°
New York	sunny and cold	45°	7°
Honolulu		90°	32°
San Francisco	foggy and cool		
Tokyo	cloudy and warm		
San Salvador		84°	29°
Mexico City		90°	32°

Unit 10
Get It Across
B

11 Look and listen.

12 Practice.

Student 1: What's the weather in Los Angeles?
Student 2: It's sunny and warm.
Student 1: What's the temperature?
Student 2: It's 75° Fahrenheit.
Student 1: What's that in Celsius?
Student 2: 24°.

13 Ask your partner for the missing information.

City	Weather	Temperature	
		Fahrenheit	Celsius
Los Angeles	sunny and warm	75°	24°
New York		45°	7°
Honolulu	cloudy and hot		
San Francisco		63°	17°
Tokyo		75°	24°
San Salvador	cloudy and warm		
Mexico City	sunny and hot	90°	32°

Unit 10
Check It

14 Circle the correct letters.

1. a. hot
   b. warm
   c. cool
   d. cold

2. a. hot
   b. warm
   c. cool
   d. cold

3. a. windy
   b. smoggy
   c. raining
   d. cloudy

4. a. smoggy
   b. foggy
   c. sunny
   d. cloudy

5. a. hot and smoggy
   b. warm and cloudy
   c. cool and windy
   d. cold and raining

15 Write the correct letter on the line.

_____ 1. Monday
_____ 2. Tuesday
_____ 3. Wednesday
_____ 4. Thursday
_____ 5. Friday
_____ 6. Saturday
_____ 7. Sunday

a. 90°F / 32°C
b. 45°F / 7°C
c. 63°F / 17°C
d. 50°F / 10°C
e. 111°F / 44°C
f. 84°F / 29°C
g. 75°F / 24°C

16 Do it.

A B C D

E F G H

I J K L

M

Q	P	O	N
U	T	S	R
Y	X	W	V
			Z

84

4	3	2	1
8	7	6	5
		10	9

88

20

30

40

50

60

70

80

90

100